Kent almost at once gives the feeling of a generous county, one with a ... soil and fine trees, with ancient villages, beautiful towns and substantial old h... on its fertility, and its natural richness has helped to keep it well car... The Romans landed here, valued these strengths, and have left su... centuries of occupation. Indeed, Kent has some of the most interesting R...

The establishment of Christianity in southern England is a theme of S... at Canterbury and founded cathedrals and churches in the county.

In the Middle Ages, four of the (five) Cinque Ports were in Kent. This federation of coastal to... formed in the 11th century, and obtained over-generous privileges from the Crown, especially of trade, in return for promises to defend Kent in times of trouble.

The threat of invasion, real or imagined, has bequeathed to us some fascinating castles and defences, dating from Roman times almost to the present. But nowadays foreign visitors arrive unthreatened, perhaps at Folkestone through the Channel Tunnel, and Kent's coastal fortresses are there to be explored and enjoyed.

It is perhaps not easy to visualise today, but in Roman times the north-eastern tip of Kent was the Isle of Thanet, separated from the mainland by a wide channel stretching from Reculver in the north to Pegwell Bay in the east. The steady silting up of the Wantsum Channel caused the decline of several places important in Roman and mediaeval times.

One of Kent's attractions is undoubtedly that, apart from the important industries connected with ship-building on the Medway, it largely escaped the Industrial Revolution of the 18th and 19th centuries.

Charles Dickens, the early Victorian novelist, came to live in this apparently peaceful world and develop his social-reforming ideas. He is associated with several Kentish towns, especially Rochester and Broadstairs, where his ideas and things familiar to him may still be explored.

So Kent's towns remained market centres and its villages rural in the 19th century, increasingly enjoyed as retreats from London. Hop-growing may no longer be a major industry but Kent continues to be a county in which the countryside, with its rural occupations and wooded landscapes, is a very strong attraction. Kent also has a great variety of building materials, lending delightful diversity to town and village.

We hope you will enjoy Kent through this guidebook, which divides into two areas: Canterbury and the East, and Western Kent.

CANTERBURY AND EASTERN KENT

Canterbury is one of the most historic cities in England. It is a glorious place to relax in beautiful surroundings, stroll down ancient streets with restricted traffic, and enjoy some interesting sights. It also has a long history of hospitality: after Archbishop Thomas Becket was murdered here in 1170, Canterbury became the leading centre for pilgrimages in England, and it remains a city friendly to visitors.

St Augustine's Abbey is perhaps the place to start. Sent by Pope Gregory the Great to re-establish Christianity in southern England, Saint Augustine came to Kent where he was welcomed by its king and queen, Ethelbert and Bertha, at their capital in Canterbury. Here he established the first English cathedral, and then his monastery in 598, where he built three small churches in a row. The middle one was dedicated to Saints Peter and Paul and became the burial ground for 7th and 8th century Kentish kings and the early archbishops, including Augustine himself. Abbot Wulfric built a remarkable rotunda linking two of the churches in about 1050.

What is now visible of these early

structures *(photo below)* is the result of excavation, since a much larger church was built here after the Norman Conquest. So venerated were Saint Augustine's churches that Abbot Scolland thought it wise to obtain the Pope's permission before demolishing them. The ruins of his 11th-century abbey remain,

with chunks of Tudor brickwork: part of Henry VIII's conversion of it into a royal palace, which survived into the 1690s. Nowadays only the two fine 14th-century gateways facing on to Monastery Street are relatively complete.

Canterbury Cathedral *(photo pages 4-5)* has turrets and pinnacles which can be glimpsed from all over the city. The most attractive approach to it is down Mercery Lane *(photo centre)*, which is narrow and overhung with bow windows and projecting upper storeys, and gives a skewed view to the west towers.

Interrupting this vista is the open space of the Butter Market, in front of Christ Church Gate *(photo left)*, which dates from 1517 and has excellent stone carvings, gothic and renaissance in style. It is the main entrance to the Cathedral and its Close.

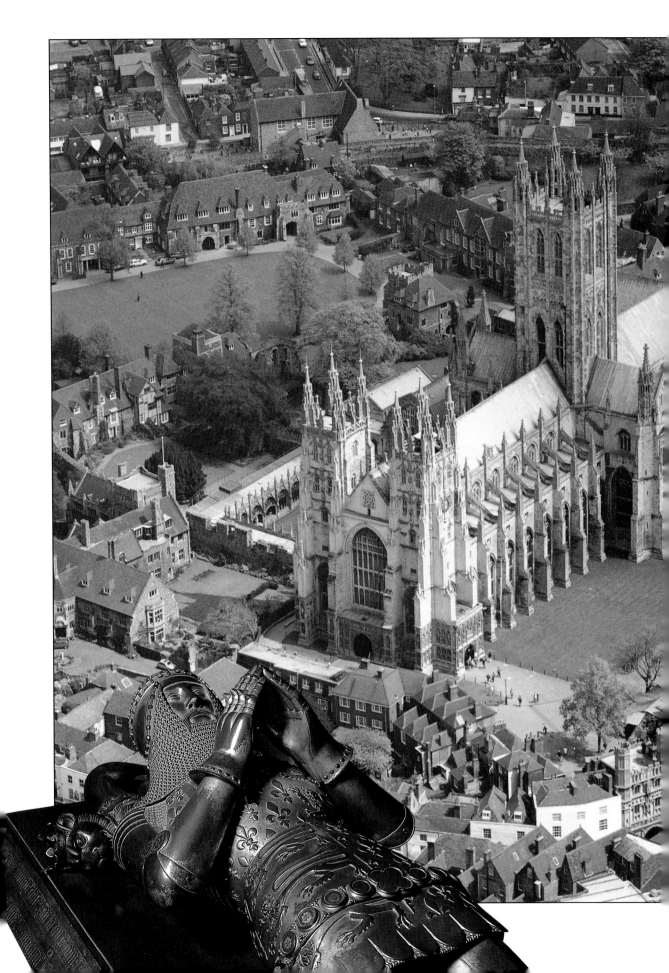

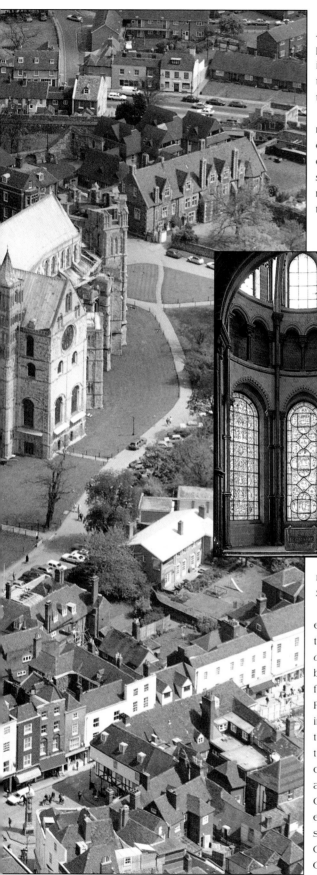

Nothing remains of St Augustine's cathedral and the present one was begun in 1070, its stylistic diversity bound together by the glorious central tower, Bell Harry, completed in 1503. That the Cathedral is so magnificent is at least partly owing to the generous offerings of mediaeval pilgrims at the shrine of St Thomas, who was murdered in the north west transept.

The earliest part of the Cathedral is the Norman crypt under the choir, with spiralling columns and carved capitals. The cloisters, with their vaulting, date from about 1400 and are some of the loveliest in England. Well beyond them lies the Norman staircase, built to a very grand design in the 1150s. Originally it led to a guest hall, the surviving part of which now belongs to The King's School.

Within the Cathedral, look out especially for the stained glass in the choir and further east (*photo above*), dating from the years before and after 1200, which was fortunate to survive the Reformation and is of exceptional interest; also for fine tombs and those of the famous, including the Black Prince, with a gilded copper effigy of 1376 (*photo left*), and Henry IV, in the Trinity Chapel. Archbishops are still enthroned in a mediaeval marble seat known as Saint Augustine's Chair, its canopy carved by Grinling Gibbons in 1704.

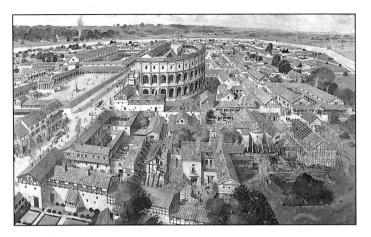

Above: Roman
Canterbury, about
AD 300, view looking
north. Canterbury
Roman Museum

Close to the Cathedral in Butchery Lane is the new Roman Museum; an exciting mix of excavated real objects: authentic reconstruction and preserved remains of a Roman town house.

The High Street and its continuation St Peter's Street are very delightful with their charmingly varied buildings. Spare forty minutes to enjoy the 'Canterbury Tales' (photo below), a spirited audio-visual evocation of Chaucer's 14th-century stories with their convincing settings, in St Margaret's Street. Take a stroll down Stour Street and enjoy the river and public gardens and the remains of the mediaeval Greyfriars, to Canterbury Heritage, the museum of the city, housed in 14th-century splendour .

St Peter's Street ends at the West Gate, the noble defence which controlled the road to London with its own drawbridge, and still impedes the traffic. Built of Kentish ragstone, it dates from 1380 and now houses a museum of local warfare.

This is the only surviving Gate to the City Walls (photo page 7), which were built of flint and stone, mainly in the 14th century. They are extensive, with many bastions, and are displayed along the southern and eastern inner ring road; the ruins of the Norman Castle rise behind them close to the Castle Street roundabout.

Above: The West Gate and Guildhall

Left: The Old Weaver's House

Below: Blackfriars Refectory, part of a Dominican friary

Above: The Canterbury Pendant, Canterbury Heritage Museum

Left: Interior of Canterbury Cathedral showing the Chancel and Presbyterium, High Altar, Trinity Chapel and the Corona

Reculver Church once looked across to the Isle of Thanet. It survives as a ruin with twin towers (*photo below*), which were kept as a landmark for shipping when the rest was demolished in 1805 - they were then still crowned with spires. The Church is, however, very historic, having been founded by St Augustine. The Roman fort in which he built it has partly been eroded by the sea, bringing the 12th century towers dramatically to the cliff edge.

For recreation Thanet, known as Kent's Leisure Coast, would make a good centre, with many activities available. Margate Bay (*photo page 9*), with its sandy beach and harbour with little boats, is very inviting.

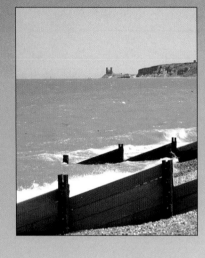

Margate has varied attractions for visitors, some of them underground. The town originated as a fishing village, of which traces remain, including the handsomely timbered Tudor house in King Street (*photo below*) with its hipped roof and overhang on all sides. Development as a seaside resort began in 1769 with Cecil Square and 18th-century Margate stretches above and below it. The bathing machine, a hut that can be wheeled into the sea, had been invented by a local resident in 1753, and encouraged the fashionable to come here.

The Shell Grotto (Grotto Hill) has a series of underground passages and chambers lined with an enormous number of sea shells forming floral panels in the style of 1800 but claimed by its owners to be prehistoric. Nearby are Margate Caves (Northdown Road), an impressive chain of tall man-made caverns carved into the chalk. Further inland stands Drapers Windmill (College Road) built in

1845 and restored to working order in 1975, and occasionally open to view.

Broadstairs was also a settlement based on farming and fishing, until 1790. The resort was developed on a steep hill leading to a beautiful sandy bay at the base of chalk cliffs (main photo and front cover). But it was the tranquillity and its reputation for healthy air that drew Charles Dickens to write some of his best books here between 1837, when he was 25, and 1851.

He rented various houses, ending up at Bleak House on the cliff, then a much smaller Regency house, surrounded by fields. Here he entertained friends such as Hans Christian Anderson and Wilkie Collins. It now displays a collection of his possessions and associated relics, such as letters and his monogrammed cutlery (photo left). Downstairs there is also a museum of shipwrecked items recovered from the Goodwin Sands, some from ships sunk in the great storm of 1703.

Nearby is the Dickens House Museum (Victoria Parade) where Mary Strong lived. Dickens used to visit the old lady, and based David Copperfield's aunt, Betsey Trotwood, on her character; the front room has been furnished to accord exactly as possible with her parlour. The house (photo below), created in about 1800 by knocking two cottages together, is very redolent of Dickens and is furnished with innumerable objects recalling his life and times, some of which belonged to him.

Ramsgate is another popular resort, with chalk cliffs and a harbour with fishing boats and private vessels *(photo below)*. At its heart is still the Regency and Early Victorian sea-bathing town. Visit the Model Village (for children) and Motor Museum, both in the Westcliff area.

A little further down the coast is Pegwell Bay and the Sandwich Bay Nature Reserve. This is a habitat unique in Kent with 1100 acres of tidal mudflats, beach, dunes and saltmarsh *(main photo)*; it is rich in lime, which promotes a particular, but diverse, range of wildlife, some of it very unusual. Pegwell is also where Hengist and

Horsa landed in 449, an event commemorated by the startling sight of a Viking longship, paddled here from Denmark in 1949.

In Roman times, Richborough, or Rutupiae as it was then called, was on a small island south of Thanet, but it now stands two miles inland. It stands on raised ground and Dickens would have enjoyed its peace. The Romans began their invasion of England here in AD 43 and Watling Street led from its west entrance. It was to become a port and commercial centre famous throughout the Roman Empire for its oysters. Richborough still has colossal Roman walls, up to eight metres high, and substantial ditches. There is a good English Heritage audio tape and museum of finds.

As Richborough declined, Sandwich took on its mantle, becoming a port by the 7th century, England's main export centre for wool in the 13th century, and one of the Cinque Ports. But its harbour, in turn, silted up in the 15th century. Its present picturesque qualities derive from its ancient wealth, the river, narrow curving streets, and varied building materials, especially timber framing and mellow brickwork. Sandwich is particularly rich in early buildings of yellow brick.

At the top of the town is the handsomely arcaded Norman tower of St Clement's Church. Lower down and facing on to the Town Quay are the Barbican, with 16th-century chequerwork bastions (photo above left) and the 14th- and 16th-century Fisher Gate, surviving from the town's defences. Enjoy a short cruise on the Stour with the Rutupiae, leaving from the quay (photo left).

Sandwich was always a centre of milling and one 18th-century smock mill survives, the White Mill (photo above) to the west. It is now fully restored, with its machinery intact, and the lower parts double as a well-presented folk museum. The miller's cottage is also shown, furnished in period style.

Walmer Castle (*photo left*) was built in 1539 against a possible French invasion, which the Pope was promoting: Henry VIII ordered its construction at high speed, but the only real action it has seen was in the Civil War. Since 1708 it has been continually adapted as the official residence of the Lord Warden of the Cinque Posts, a post historically given to distinguished people. Walmer houses many mementoes of them, including William Pitt's desk, and the Duke of Wellington's Room has been reconstructed from old pictures: his campaign bed and wellington boots are among many items on show. Visitors also see the dining and drawing rooms of the first female Warden, the late HM The Queen Mother.

To understand what a slightly more elaborate version of Walmer looked

like when new, visit Deal Castle (*photo below*), the largest and most complete of Henry VIII's extraordinary coastal defences. It was the middle one of the three built to defend the safe anchorage known as The Downs, inshore of the Goodwin Sands (the third has been all but swallowed by the sea). Deal Castle was then the latest thing in warfare, with a geometrical plan giving five tiers of artillery with 145 gunports for all-round fire. Stone from monasteries destroyed by King Henry was used in its construction, but much of the interior was created in Tudor brick.

Dover is, by its position, a keystone in our defences and part of the history of England, with ramparts which date back to the Iron Age. The Castle (*photos on page 14*), one of our largest, was built mainly in the 12th and 13th centuries by

Henry II and Henry III and covers the whole hill-top. It encloses possibly the oldest building in England, a Roman lighthouse built in the 1st century AD – of which a surprising amount remains – and has wonderful views. Below it are the extensive tunnels known as Hellfire Corner, dug into the White Cliffs in the 12th century, and during the Napoleonic troubles and the Second World War: they included the Allied Command Headquarters created in 1941-43.

Dover's past is interestingly presented by Dover Museum. One of its exhibits, in the Bronze Age Boat Gallery, is a 3,550-year-old sea-going vessel, the oldest known in the world and discovered in Dover in 1922. While here, visit also the nearby Roman Painted House, a hotel for official visitors, with lively and colourful wall paintings.

For something more up-to-date, the Eurotunnel Exhibition Centre at Folkestone (*photo page 15*) will satisfy all curiosity about how we were recently joined to France and show you the equipment used. It is a huge display, with a history of the previous attempts to build tunnels since 1802 and why they failed, until the present one which was started in 1987 and declared open in 1994. There is the option of a guided bus-tour of the Terminal.

The perfect contrast to Eurotunnel must be Lympne Castle, which is really a 14th-century fortified house and a charming building of mellow stone with commanding views over Romney Marsh. It is still privately owned and restoration in the 20th century has returned it close to its mediaeval form, with some sensitive additions. Mr Margary's furnishings and collections add an individual touch which makes a visit more memorable.

To its east lies the ancient town of Hythe *(photo page 14)*, its period of prosperity as a Cinque Port being the 12th and 13th centuries. Of this, the church is now the principal reminder and it has a curious vault filled with human bones. Modern Hythe is a centre for recreation such as fishing and windsurfing, and the terminus of the tiny Romney, Hythe and Dymchurch steam railway which chugs for only 14 miles across Romney Marsh.

Chilham village's attraction is mainly that of ancient buildings enjoyed as scenery *(photo right)*, although it is hardly more than an irregularly shaped square. But it has a wonderful mixture of substantial timber-framed houses and later brick ones, offset by the twin lodges of a 17th-century brick 'castle' on one side and the splendid Church tower on the other. There are curving streets leading away and downhill from the four corners, with further intriguing views.

Faversham is one of the most attractive towns

in Kent to explore, its historic centre partly pedestrianised and made attractive to visitors. Start by the pump *(photo below left)* and 17th-century Guildhall with its columns and stroll in all directions: there is much to see. The Heritage Centre in Preston Street has good suggestions for walks and any amount of historical information.

Faversham is a bright town with much good architectural detail from the Middle Ages onwards; buildings large and small, urbane and picturesque, delight the eye both individually and as groups. The parish church looks at first sight mainly mediaeval but has a fine openwork spire dating from 1799 and a classical nave built in 1755.

Since the 16th century Faversham has been at the centre of our gunpowder industry, which has blown up parts of it occasionally, and only one set of mills remains. The 18th-century Chart Mills, powered by the Westbrook, are the oldest of their kind in the world and still have their machinery intact; Nelson's powder was made here and their exterior is on view, and sometimes the interior.

WEST KENT

The cannon balls discharged by Nelson's powder (*see page 15*) were carved nearby, from Kentish ragstone cut from quarries at Maidstone, now the county town. Near the town centre and overlooking the Medway is the old Archbishop's Palace (*photo above*), dating from the late Middle Ages when the Palace was in the heart of Maidstone. Nearby is the magnificent 15th-century Archbishops' Tithe Barn (*photo right*) with its crown-post roof, now home to the very fine Tyrwhitt-Drake Museum of Carriages. This exceptional collection is augmented with others on loan from the Queen. The mediaeval Palace 'Gatehouse' has 14th-century windows and is now the Tourist Information Centre.

On the north side of Maidstone is the Museum of Kent Life at Cobtree (*photo*

(*above*). Here are presented some of the realities of living in the Kent countryside, with its many industries, over the last 200 years. Examples of equipment and explanations of their use make an interesting and appropriate display in the old farm buildings. Cobtree may be Charles Dickens' Dingley Dell of the *Pickwick Papers* and as an estate was given to Maidstone in 1964 by Sir Gerald Tyrwhitt-Drake.

Within easy reach of Maidstone are two very different houses. Leeds Castle (*photo below and on front cover*) is a well-developed venue, with its maze, aviary, grotto, gardens and the lakes with their black swans, all most attractively presented. The castle is a spectacular sight. It is surrounded by a wooded landscape shelving down to a large lake with two islands, upon which it stands. The castle belonged to the king throughout the Middle Ages and the buildings are mainly mediaeval.

What particularly brings them to life is the restoration made by Lady Baillie who devoted herself to the castle, in 1926. She was then only 26 and made good use of her inheritance from her American (Whitney) mother. The interior is not to be missed, fitted and furnished with Lady Baillie's sure eye for what was appropriate, and there are some lovely tapestries. It is now run by a charitable trust which organises many events here.

Boughton Monchelsea Place (*photo below right*) is still a family house in a

deer park, furnished in an unselfconscious manner with the accumulated possessions of generations of owners. It is Elizabethan, but has a fine staircase and three Mortlake tapestries dating from the mid-17th century. The ground floor rooms and the main front were given elegant gothic features in the Regency period.

Between Maidstone and Rochester lies Aylesford *(main photo)*, one of Kent's historic villages. It has great charm, with its 14th-century bridge over the Medway, built of Kentish ragstone, narrow streets and Norman church on the hill. There is a splendid timber-framed inn with two overhanging storeys, and a Carmelite friary.

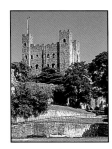

Rochester is an ancient city with a compact historic spine centring on the High Street. It has many things worth seeing, including the Guildhall and its excellent museum, also the 15th-century Chertsey's Gate. This leads to the Cathedral (*photo below*) whose nave is mid-12th century. It has a good west front with carvings and sculpture, while the eastern arms are early gothic, pleasantly shafted with marble. Rochester is our second oldest see, founded by St Augustine soon after the year 600.

Rochester is dominated by its castle (*photo right*), built to protect Watling Street's river crossing, and giving marvellously extensive views of the Medway and its shipping. The great tower, built in about 1130, is much better preserved within than its gaunt exterior suggests and has some Norman fire-places, some of the earliest in England, with chevron mouldings.

Charles Dickens knew Rochester well and it features throughout his works, as Rochester in *Pickwick Papers* and under various disguises elsewhere. Eastgate

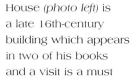

House (*photo left*) is a late 16th-century building which appears in two of his books and a visit is a must for every Dickens enthusiast. Dickens World at Chatham provides a wealth of fun and interest for all ages (*photo front cover*).

Dickens's father worked in the cashier's office at Chatham Dockyard, an astonishing relic of English naval history. Queen Elizabeth started constructing our warships here, but the architecture of the Dockyard reflects the 18th century more than any other and so is unique.

Modern technology has been employed to help interpret the past practices of building and fitting out ships on this great campus, and the result is an enjoyable insight into centuries-old crafts and traditions. Not all the buildings can be entered, but few will want to spend less than half a day here. The

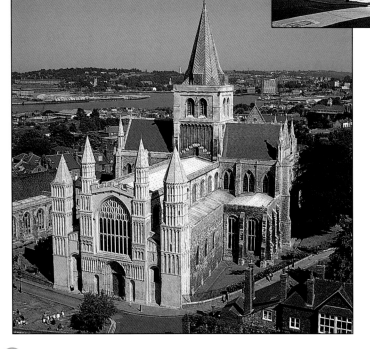

them, but elsewhere the fort's role in the Second World War is brought to life.

One of the few successful conquests of England is commemorated in Lullingstone Roman Villa, somewhat to the west of Chatham. This villa or farmhouse is one of the finest in England and had a bathing suite - for relaxation not cleanliness - and a household shrine.

The villa remained in use, being enlarged occasionally, for about 340 years. Two of its later features are good multi-coloured mosaics of mythological subjects and geometrical designs. The English Heritage displays and audio-tape enliven this interesting site.

Below: Rochester

18th-century Ropework building alone is a quarter of a mile long (*photo above*).

Fort Amherst was built in 1756 to protect the Dockyard, but it was so greatly extended by the hard work of French prisoners that it is now mainly of the Napoleonic period. Storehouses have always been hidden underground here and much of the fort is subterranean. Some of the barrack rooms have been restored to the condition in which Wellington's men knew

Ightham Mote is a picturesque old manor house built of stone, also timber-framing, brick, plaster and tile, reflected in its moat *(photos left & below)*, which has duck and dragonfly in their season. It is also a house of considerable architectural interest, carefully researched and restored by the National Trust, and built mainly in the 14th and 15th centuries.

It is all that an authentic mediaeval house should be, with a gatehouse and great hall, gallery and chapels, rooms open to their roofs, panelling and oak ceilings, and large fireplaces. The house was given to the Trust and the furniture collected by Charles Henry Robinson, from New England, who fell in love with Ightham Mote as a young man and bought it many years later after a successful career.

The distant impression of the mighty house of Knole *(photo above, top)* is almost of a town, with a roofscape of turrets and gables, battlements, chimneys, finials and heraldic beasts, set within an ancient deer-park. It is perhaps best described as an early 17th-century private palace, created by Thomas Sackville, first Earl of Dorset, within the late mediaeval shell of a palace built by the archbishops of Canterbury.

Knole has one of the most perfect early 17th century interiors in Europe, with its staircases, ceilings, fireplaces and panelling. The furnishings are a treasure-house of the 17th century and unusually magnificent; some are from royal collections, and there is both ebony and silver furniture, and tapestries as bright as the day they were woven.

Sevenoaks is an attractive town *(photo left)*, especially the High Street, with some of its best buildings close to Knole's gates.

Chartwell *(photo page 24)* is almost the opposite of Knole, a moderate-sized house devoted to one modern man, Sir Winston Churchill. Chartwell, originally Tudor, was largely rebuilt for him as his main home in 1923 and his recreations of painting, writing history books and building brick walls can all be appreciated here. Among the contents are his collection of Napoleonic relics, his state robes, political cartoons and gifts from statesmen around the world.

The Castle at Tonbridge *(photo below)* was built to guard a ford on the Medway. Its gatehouse is unusually handsome for military architecture and built of a particularly beautiful stone; in the principal rooms the windows and fireplaces also have finely carved details. But it was not all for show: the gatehouse is very strongly designed, with more than the usual number of portcullises, and the front of its towers are peppered with the small scars of futile bullets.

Royal Tunbridge Wells grew up as a spa and owes its development to the visits of royalty and fashionable society in the 17th and 18th centuries. This was the town's heyday, when the well-to-do came to seek husbands for their daughters, while taking the waters and attending the coffee-houses and balls. The social scene was organised by the dandy, Beau Nash, who made sure everyone adhered to his 'rules' of social behaviour.

At its heart is The Pantiles (*photo left*) which, together with its continuous colonnade, dates from the 17th century; it is named after its original paving, long since replaced with stone. At one end of this walk is the chalybeate spring (*photo above*), where you may drink the water, and beyond it is the Church of King Charles the Martyr, which is late 17th century and has some very fine plasterwork.

Left: A Georgian costumed event

Penshurst Place (*photo below*) is one of England's great country houses, and the Sidney family lives there as they have done since 1552. At its core is a remarkably well-preserved manor house with its famous great hall, built for a lord mayor of London in 1341, and enlarged in the 15th and 16th centuries. It was the home of the romantic 16th-century soldier and poet Sir Philip Sidney. The house is furnished with portraits and other family treasures acquired over the centuries.

At Chiddingstone Castle there is an older mansion remodelled in the Regency gothic style, hence the name 'Castle'. What is most remarkable about it

is the interior, which is partly furnished for living, and partly as a private museum housing the collections of its last owner, Denys Bower. These are of Buddhist, Japanese, Egyptian, Jacobite and Stuart works of art, and makes a visit to this house more surprising than most.

Opposite the church is the small but very picturesque village *(photo below)*. It is scarcely more than a group of timber-framed buildings, but they are substantial and eye-catching, as the best Kentish ones often are. Behind them is the Chiding Stone *(photo left)*, a rounded knob of sandstone projecting from the living rock. It presumably gave its name, which goes back to at least the 12th century, to the village, but what it means is less certain; legend says it was a preaching place in use before the church was built.

Hever Castle (photo right) is small and moated, and although externally faced with stone, the courtyard is rather charmingly timber-framed. One of Henry VIII's queens, Anne Boleyn grew up here. In 1903, W. W. Astor applied his money and energy to enhancing the old castle, bringing in old and new materials and the best craftsmen. The result combines American panache with English design and workmanship, and even the portcullis are in working order. The same lavishness and care went into obtaining the finest and most appropriate furnishings, a remarkable number of which are associated with Henry and Anne. A visit is an experience not to be missed.

The Hop Farm at Beltring (photos below) surely has the largest group of oast houses anywhere in England.

In the 16th century Beltring belonged to Queen Elizabeth I's apothecary and in the late 19th century E. A. White, a great improver of hops, rented it and built most of the present oast houses.

The farm buildings now house various country attractions, the most appropriate of them the informative display on the hop industry, and there are some fine shire horses.

The garden at Scotney Castle is very long-established and occupies a hillside between the early Victorian house at the top and the old castle in its broad moat. It is skilfully laid out to give ever-changing views, not only through the garden itself, but into the estate with its woodland, ponds, parkland and meadows. The 14th-century castle *(photo right)*, which was enlarged and remained a family house, was partly demolished in 1843 to enhance its picturesque qualities, and the result is the prettiest place imaginable. The planting scheme, which gives colour and interest throughout the year, is also calculated to interest the serious gardener.

Sissinghurst Castle's garden is one of the most famous in England, and its popularity has led to the introduction of a timed-entry system. Vita Sackville-West (from Knole) and Harold Nicolson bought the site with its Elizabethan brick buildings in 1930 and cleverly cultivated six acres around them. There are ten 'rooms', linked or separated in various ways, all different, and now mature. Visitors also see part of their house and Vita's study in the tower.

Biddenden Vineyard *(photo right)* is the oldest of several in Kent. Admittance is free and you may walk through the vineyard and the buildings where processing takes place, and into the shop to sample their products. Several varieties of white wine and cider are made, and visitors account for a large proportion of their sales. But do not leave Biddenden without also seeing one of Kent's prettiest village streets *(photo left)*.

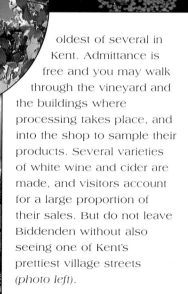

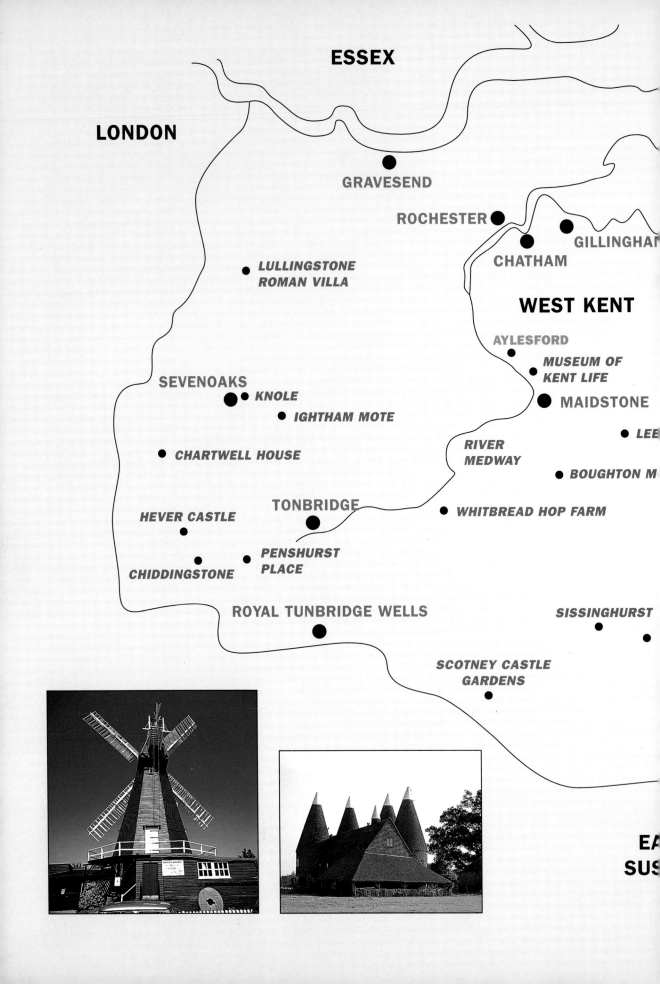

ESSEX

LONDON

GRAVESEND

ROCHESTER

GILLINGHAM

CHATHAM

WEST KENT

LULLINGSTONE
ROMAN VILLA

AYLESFORD

MUSEUM OF
KENT LIFE

SEVENOAKS

KNOLE

MAIDSTONE

IGHTHAM MOTE

LEE

CHARTWELL HOUSE

RIVER
MEDWAY

BOUGHTON M

TONBRIDGE

WHITBREAD HOP FARM

HEVER CASTLE

PENSHURST
PLACE

CHIDDINGSTONE

ROYAL TUNBRIDGE WELLS

SISSINGHURST

SCOTNEY CASTLE
GARDENS

EA
SUS